P9-CEO-285

621.4
W

Weiss   C1

AUTHOR

Motors and engines

TITLE

and how they work

621.4   6391
W   C1

    Weiss

        Motors and engines and
    how they work

GALLINAS SCHOOL
177 NORTH SAN PEDRO RD.
SAN RAFAEL, CA. 94903

**MOTORS and
ENGINES and How They Work**

LIBRARY
~~Santa Venetia School~~
~~San Rafael, Calif.~~

GALLINAS SCHOOL
177 NORTH SAN PEDRO RD.
SAN RAFAEL, CA. 94903

MOTORS and ENGINES and How They Work

By Harvey Weiss

Illustrated

Thomas Y. Crowell Company, New York

The author wishes to thank the following organizations for their generous assistance in the preparation of this book: the Lick Observatory, the Westinghouse Corporation, the National Aeronautics and Space Administration, the United States Air Force, the Ford Motor Company, the United States Navy, the Union Pacific Railroad, the Netherlands National Tourist Office, Pearson Yachts, the Smithsonian Institution, the U. S. Bureau of Reclamation, and Ewing Galloway, New York.

6391

COPYRIGHT © 1969 by HARVEY WEISS

All rights reserved. Except for use in a review, the reproduction or utilization of this work in any form or by any electronic, mechanical, or other means, now known or hereafter invented, including xerography, photocopying, and recording, and in any information storage and retrieval system is forbidden without the written permission of the publisher.

MANUFACTURED IN THE UNITED STATES OF AMERICA

L. C. Card 69-11828

1 2 3 4 5 6 7 8 9 10

CONTENTS

MOTORS and
ENGINES and How They Work

WHAT IS AN ENGINE?

Late one afternoon I sat down and tried to think of how many motors and engines I had seen or used in the course of that day. There were so many that I finally lost count.

First was the alarm clock that woke me up in the morning. That has two engines inside: a spring engine that turns the hands on the face of the clock, and another that makes the alarm sound. Then, there was a little electric motor in the electric shaver I used. The electric toothbrush had a motor that made it work. When I opened the door of my refrigerator, the eggs and juice and milk I took out were fresh and cold because there was an electric motor, purring away, driving the cooling apparatus. The car I drove was powered by a gasoline engine. And as I drove by a river, I saw a boat. It was a sailboat, and its sails were really a sort of wind engine.

1

Clocks, fans, air-conditioners, heating systems, buses, airplanes, boats, trucks, and so on and on—we are, in fact, surrounded by an enormous number of different kinds of motors and engines. The sort of life we lead today would not be possible without them. If there were no gasoline engine, we would travel by foot or by horse and carriage. Without the electric motor, we would use an icebox instead of a refrigerator. We would weave cloth and pump water by hand, and tell time by the sun, if there were no engines.

What, exactly, is an engine?

It is a machine that changes one form of energy into another form that can produce mechanical work.

Let's see how one form of energy can be changed into another form. We'll take a very simple example. Imagine a stormy day, and a hanging wooden sign flapping in the

wind. With every gust of wind the sign swings back and forth. Now suppose there is a board fence right next to this sign, and a loose nail is sticking out of it. After a few minutes of swinging and banging, the nail will be driven into the fence—just as if you had been hitting it with a hammer.

Now, wind is simply air in motion. And even the wildest wind in a fierce hurricane would not, by itself, be able to drive a nail into even the softest wood. The wind needs a tool with which to do its work—and that, of course, is the swinging sign.

The sign is actually a kind of engine. It has taken one form of energy, the wind, and changed it into a different form of energy: a hammering action. Energy has been used to do work. And this is exactly the sort of thing that all the engines described in this book do. The gasoline engine takes the explosive energy that is stored in gasoline and changes it into the energy that turns the wheels of a car. The steam engine takes the energy in steam and changes it into the energy that drives a locomotive.

There are many different kinds of energy. There is the energy stored in a piece of wood that can be burned. There is energy in a flowing river, a lump of coal, an electric battery. Atomic scientists are learning how to use the energy that is contained in the simplest and most common materials.

Each kind of energy can be used only by means of its own special kind of engine. There are engines that use electricity, engines that use the wind, engines that use gravity, and so on. One of the simplest engines uses water —so let's look at that one first.

This old water mill was built in 1798. Water from a mountain stream is conducted by means of a wooden chute, or "flume," to a point directly over the top of the water wheel. You can see the water flowing out of the flume and onto the wheel.

WATER ENGINES

With the exception of some desert areas, water is found in all parts of the world. So it is not surprising that man, from earliest times, has tried to use the energy it contains. The movement and weight of water are taken advantage of by engines that are generally wheel shaped. In fact, the more simple types of water engines are called *water wheels*. In the illustration below, you can see how a water wheel operates. The wheel is placed in such a position that the stream of water falls onto the blades of the wheel. The weight of the water presses down on the blades, forcing the wheel to turn. Thus, the energy of the

falling water has been changed to the energy of the turning wheel.

There is another kind of water wheel that uses the *motion* of flowing water, rather than the *weight* of falling water. It is shown below. In this case the water, rushing downstream, pushes against the blades on the bottom of the wheel, causing it to turn.

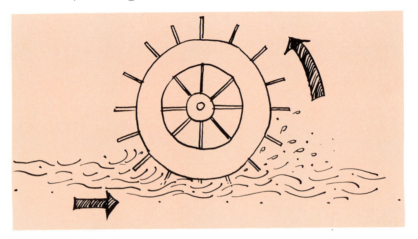

With both of these wheels we end up with a turning force. But a big wheel just turning around and around isn't doing any useful work—even though it may look very pretty. The simplest way to get some practical use out of a water wheel is shown below. A grindstone is fastened to one end of the axle. As the wheel turns, the grindstone turns. Now, the water wheel will provide the energy to sharpen a knife or an axe blade.

The flowing water in a stream is like the blowing wind mentioned in the last chapter. The wind couldn't hammer a nail, nor could the water sharpen a knife—until some device was added to change the energy into a usable form.

Can you think of any other ways in which the turning motion could be used? A few possibilities are shown below.

If you need more than a simple turning motion to do a job, a slightly more complicated device is required. The crank is the simplest way of changing a rotating motion to a back-and-forth, or push-pull, motion. This type of movement can be used to raise and lower a pump handle, or push a saw blade back and forth.

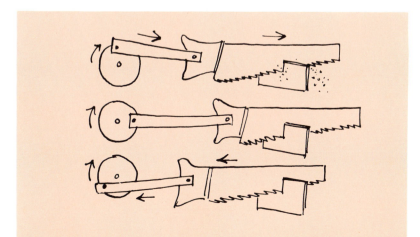

Primitive water wheels were most often put to use for grinding flour. Two heavy, flat millstones served this purpose. The lower millstone remained stationary, and the upper millstone was turned by the water wheel with a simple gear arrangement. The rough grain was poured into the hole in the upper stone. It sifted down into the space between the two stones and was ground into a fine powder, which was forced out at the edges. This was collected, bagged, and used in baking.

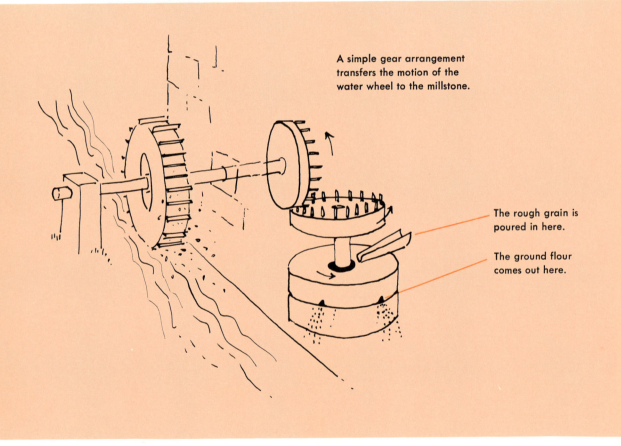

A simple gear arrangement transfers the motion of the water wheel to the millstone.

The rough grain is poured in here.

The ground flour comes out here.

HOW TO MAKE A MODEL WATER WHEEL

It is not difficult to make a simple water wheel yourself, which will show what this kind of engine is like in actual motion.

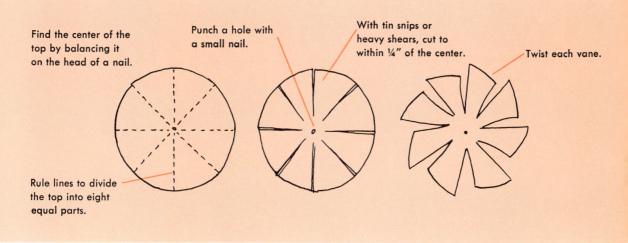

Find the center of the top by balancing it on the head of a nail.

Rule lines to divide the top into eight equal parts.

Punch a hole with a small nail.

With tin snips or heavy shears, cut to within ¼" of the center.

Twist each vane.

Cut off the top of a tin can. Get a pair of tin snips or heavy shears and slice the top as shown. Then, with a nail, punch a small hole in the center. (Make sure it is the exact center.) Now bend the blades as shown. Get a stiff wire about six inches long—or you can use a straightened-out paper clip. Put the wire through the hole in the wheel and tape it in place, using adhesive tape or masking tape. Make sure the wheel is firmly attached to the wire, and not leaning or slanted.

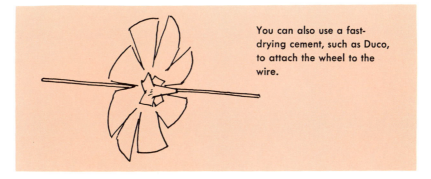

You can also use a fast-drying cement, such as Duco, to attach the wheel to the wire.

Now turn on the faucet in your kitchen or bathroom sink and put the wheel under the stream of water, holding the wire axle lightly between your fingers. Let the water strike the blades on only one half of the wheel. The wheel will spin around at a great rate. You now have a working model of a water engine.

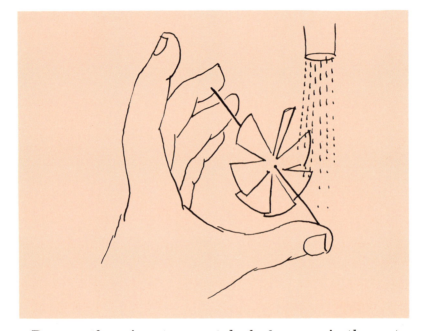

Because there is not a great deal of energy in the water coming out of a faucet, and because your engine is small and flimsy, there is not much practical work that it can do. But it will turn a little more efficiently and will look nicer if you mount it on a small block of wood. The drawing opposite shows how you can do this. If you find that the wire you are using is too stiff to bend easily, use a pair of pliers. Then you can bend the wire quite accurately.

10

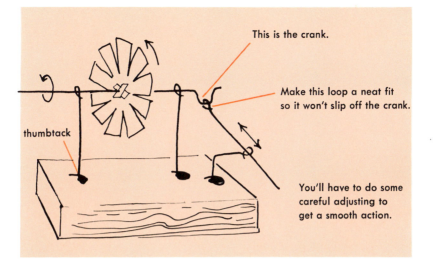

This is the crank.

Make this loop a neat fit so it won't slip off the crank.

thumbtack

You'll have to do some careful adjusting to get a smooth action.

With the water wheel mounted securely, you can do a little experimenting. Take one end of the wire on which the wheel is mounted and bend it into a "U" shape. This is now a crank. Take another short length of wire, make a small loop in one end, and fit the loop over the crank. Now, when the wheel turns, the rotating movement is changed to a back-and-forth movement.

You may also want to try fastening a piece of thread to the wire shaft to see how great a load the wheel will raise.

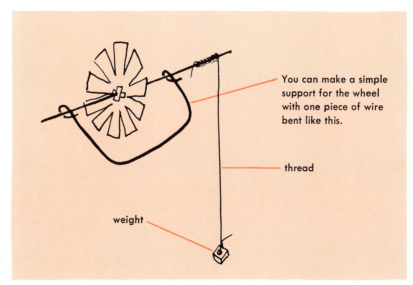

You can make a simple support for the wheel with one piece of wire bent like this.

thread

weight

This is the Shasta Dam and its powerhouse, in California. On the left you can see five pipes that carry the water down to the turbines inside the powerhouse. The water shooting out from the center of the dam is simply an excess overflow.

WATER WHEELS TODAY

Water wheels are very much in use today—but in much more complex form than the sort used to turn a millstone. Modern water wheels are enormous, carefully engineered, and precisely balanced. They are used to turn generators, which produce electricity. Many dams are built today for the sole purpose of holding back water

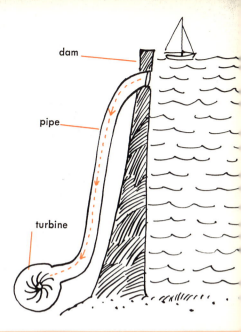

that is fed down to water wheels. It comes down in large pipes, with tremendous weight and force.

The large, modern water wheel is called a *turbine*. A turbine may not look much like the crude water wheel that is slowly turning alongside a small mountain stream; but both these wheels are water engines, and both work on exactly the same principle.

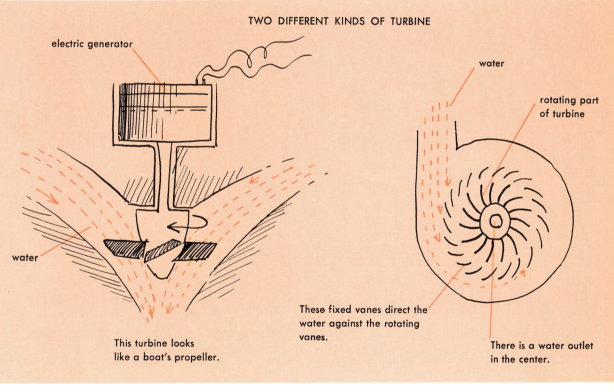

TWO DIFFERENT KINDS OF TURBINE

electric generator

water

This turbine looks like a boat's propeller.

These fixed vanes direct the water against the rotating vanes.

water

rotating part of turbine

There is a water outlet in the center.

13

This windmill in Holland is used to turn the saw blade in a lumber mill. When the mill is in operation, cloth panels are pulled down over the wooden lattice frames. These cloth "sails" catch the wind and produce a rotating movement. The entire upper part of the windmill can be turned so as to face the wind.

WIND ENGINES

Wind is another source of energy that you can find almost anywhere. It isn't quite as reliable as a river or stream or a dammed lake; but, in many places, the wind does blow in a fairly steady, dependable way.

The energy of the wind is usually harnessed by means of a wheel with blades—quite like the water wheel. However, the blades are not placed in the same way. They are positioned at an angle to the shaft, as shown in the margin. It is a fan (or propeller) type of arrangement and is placed so that it faces into the direction from which the wind is coming.

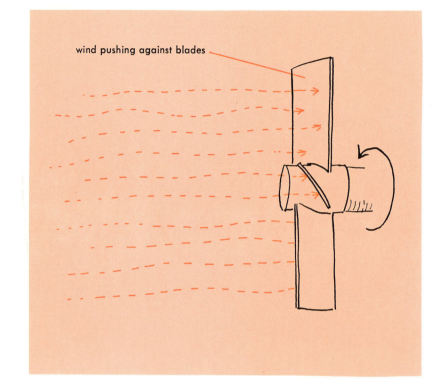

wind pushing against blades

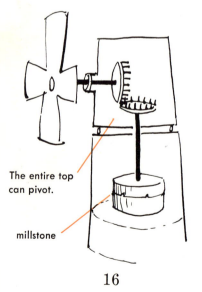

The entire top can pivot.

millstone

When wind strikes a blade of a wind engine, it exerts pressure on it—it pushes. Since the blade is firmly attached to the shaft, however, it cannot be pushed backward. It can only revolve, and we get a turning motion.

With many large blades on a carefully balanced shaft and with a steady wind blowing, a great deal of power is obtained. It is enough power to turn the sort of heavy millstone used to grind flour.

16

On many small farms far from electric power lines, windmills are still used. They are smaller than the huge Dutch windmills, but they are more efficient. Usually they are attached to a generator, which makes electricity.

SAILS

Another obvious use of wind is to propel sailboats. With a big spread of canvas and a brisk wind, a sailboat will move with speed and power. When the wind is behind

The power of the wind is being harnessed by these sails to move the boat through the water with speed and efficiency.

17

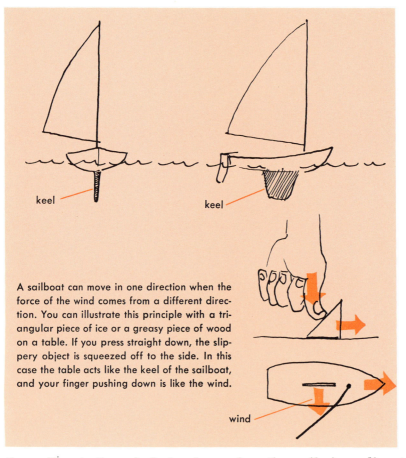

A sailboat can move in one direction when the force of the wind comes from a different direction. You can illustrate this principle with a triangular piece of ice or a greasy piece of wood on a table. If you press straight down, the slippery object is squeezed off to the side. In this case the table acts like the keel of the sailboat, and your finger pushing down is like the wind.

keel

keel

wind

the sailboat, the wind simply pushes the sails in a direct and obvious way. But have you ever wondered why a sailboat moves straight ahead even when the wind is coming from the side?

The reason is that the sails are acting like the blades on the windmill. The blades can move only sideways, rotating, because that is the only way the shaft can move. And with a sailboat, the hull moves only forward because the long, thin keel under water moves only forward. The keel acts like a knife in butter. The knife blade can move back and forth, or up and down. But you won't have much success trying to push a knife *sideways* through a bar of butter. This is just what happens with the sailboat hull. The keel is like the knife; the water is like the butter.

A MODEL SAILBOAT

You can see for yourself the way a sailboat performs if you make a little model like the one shown below. The sail is a stiff piece of paper, taped to a piece of wire or a dowel. Put the model in a dishpan of water or in the bathtub. Adjust the sail so it is at the angle shown, and then blow from the side.

Attach a keel to the boat and try blowing again. You'll see that it makes quite a difference. Without the keel the boat will simply spin about or drift sideways. With the keel it will move straight ahead—even though you are blowing from the side.

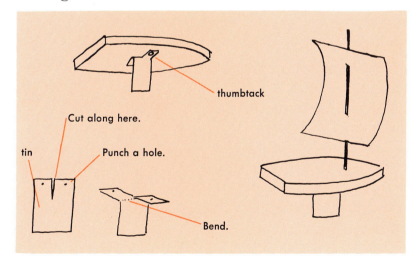

A MODEL WINDMILL

You can make a small wind engine for yourself, in much the same way you made the water wheel described in the previous chapter. All you need is the top of a tin can, a few pieces of wire or paper clips, some tape, dowels, and a block of wood for a base.

Cut the tin top as shown, and punch a small hole in the center. Twist the blades—but not as much as for the water wheel. Then attach the wheel to the shaft. Make a support for the shaft as shown.

Now, if it is a breezy day, open the window and hold your engine so that it is facing into the wind. It will spin about at a great rate. Try making a crank and connecting rod, and see how they work.

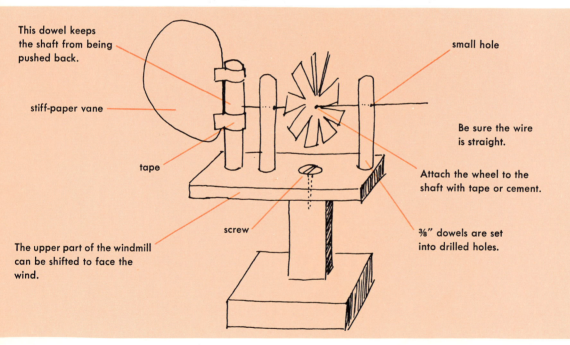

This dowel keeps the shaft from being pushed back.

stiff-paper vane

tape

The upper part of the windmill can be shifted to face the wind.

screw

small hole

Be sure the wire is straight.

Attach the wheel to the shaft with tape or cement.

⅜" dowels are set into drilled holes.

SOME OTHER WIND ENGINES YOU CAN MAKE

There are any number of ways the wind can be used as a source of energy. A few of these are illustrated below.

If you build a small sail like the one shown here, you can hold it to catch the wind when you are ice-skating or roller-skating. On a windy day you'll really scoot along.

A land sailer is not difficult to build. A pair of old roller skates, some boards, a couple of poles, an old sheet—and off you go. You could also make a simple iceboat, using old ice skate blades or strips of metal instead of roller skates.

If you are a little more ambitious and have the use of some tools, you may want to try making a fairly large wind engine like the one shown here. The blades are made of any stiff sheet metal you can find, or else ¼-inch plywood. The trickiest part of this job is the center piece: the hole must be exactly centered and exactly perpendicular. You must also be sure that the shaft, or axle, is a neat fit and properly supported so that it can easily turn. If the engine is carefully constructed, you can make a pulley arrangement that will turn a small grindstone or sanding disk on a breezy day. Or, if you have a small generator of the sort that is used on bicycles, you can use that to light a bulb.

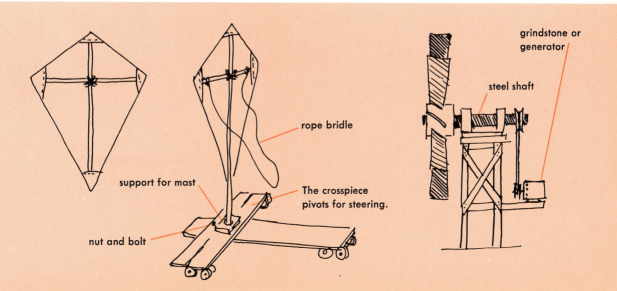

support for mast

nut and bolt

rope bridle

The crosspiece pivots for steering.

grindstone or generator

steel shaft

GRAVITY ENGINES

Gravity is the force that keeps everything on the earth from just flying off into space. It is the force that causes a stone to fall when you drop it, or a ball to roll downhill rather than uphill.

A gravity engine uses the energy *stored* in an object that is raised up. The larger and heavier the object, the more energy that is waiting and ready to go to work for you. Let's take a specific example. Suppose there were a spike sticking up out of the ground, and you dropped a small rock on it. The falling rock, striking the spike, would drive it a certain distance into the ground. But if you had a really large, heavy rock and dropped that on the spike, it would certainly drive it much deeper into the ground.

The falling rock is actually a simple gravity engine. You used the energy of your body to lift the rock. (The heavier the rock, the more energy you would have to use.) The energy was stored in the raised rock. When you released the rock, the energy was put to work on the spike.

22

There is a machine called a *pile driver*, which works on exactly the same principle as the falling rock. It is used to hammer wooden poles or steel pipes into muddy or sandy ground. These are used for the foundations of buildings or for docks, wherever a heavy construction must rest on a firm base.

The most important part of the pile driver is a very heavy piece of iron, which can slide up and down on a vertical track. Some source of energy is used to hoist this

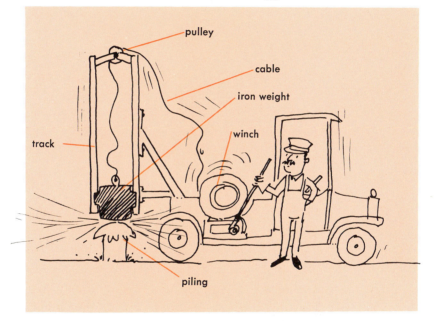

iron weight up to the top of the track; then it is released. It smacks down onto the top of the pole or pipe, again and again, gradually driving it into the ground.

Another example of a gravity engine is the *hourglass*. It is gravity that causes the little particles of sand to fall. The size of the small opening between the upper and lower halves of the hourglass is very carefully figured. How large this opening is determines how fast the sand will fall. If the space were too large, the hourglass would "run fast."

Some hourglasses actually do take an hour to let the sand go from top to bottom. These are rather large and hold a lot of sand. The more common hourglasses run for two or three minutes. These are small, and are useful for timing things like telephone calls and soft-boiled eggs.

The water engines discussed in the first chapter are, in a way, also gravity engines. This is true of the water wheel described on page 5, where the water is *falling* onto the blades of the wheel, causing it to revolve. So you might say it is the force of gravity that is causing the wheel to turn.

And as for the "undershot" water wheel shown on page 6, the rushing water of the river is flowing downstream because of the force of gravity.

24

A GRAVITY ENGINE YOU CAN BUILD

Because sand—like water—can be made to move in a steady, flowing way, you can use it to turn the sort of water wheel described on page 10. Only, now you'll have to call it a "sand wheel." The drawing below shows how it is built. If you build this engine, make sure that the sand you use is clean and dry—otherwise it will stick in the funnel. If your sand is coarse, with particles of many different sizes, you should filter it through a screen to remove the large grains or impurities.

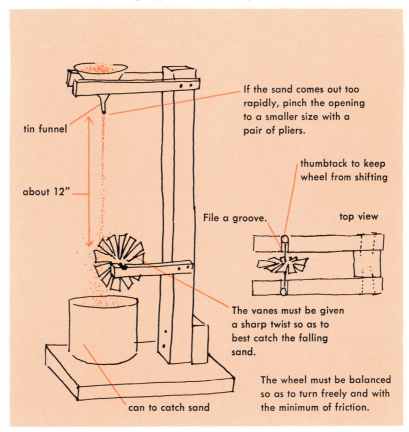

tin funnel

about 12"

If the sand comes out too rapidly, pinch the opening to a smaller size with a pair of pliers.

thumbtack to keep wheel from shifting

File a groove.

top view

The vanes must be given a sharp twist so as to best catch the falling sand.

can to catch sand

The wheel must be balanced so as to turn freely and with the minimum of friction.

25

LIBRARY
Santa Venetia School
San Rafael, Calif.

CLOCKS

Another time-telling engine that uses the force of gravity is found in the old-fashioned grandfather clock. This type of device is not what usually comes to mind when you say "engine." A grandfather clock doesn't do any heavy or strenuous work; it simply sits in a corner, gently ticktocking. But some kind of energy is needed to turn the hour and minute hands. This energy is provided by gravity, pulling down a heavy weight, as shown in the diagram below.

As the weight falls lower and lower, the string unwinds, causing the shaft to rotate. In actual practice, of course, a clock mechanism is much more complicated than this, as you must know if you have ever taken a clock apart—and then tried to put it together again!

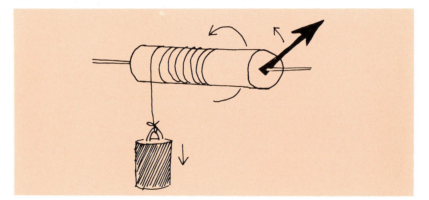

With the arrangement shown above, the weight would simply fall with a thud, and the shaft and hand would spin around a few times and then stop. The energy stored in the weight would be immediately used up. What is needed is some kind of device to slow down the fall of the weight, so that the shaft will turn very gradually, over a long period of time. Some grandfather clocks will keep running for more than a week.

A very ingenious little arrangement called an *escape mechanism* is the means by which the fall of the weight is slowed down.

This same type of escape mechanism is used in wristwatches and alarm clocks. For these, a wound-up spring rather than a raised weight provides the source of power. But there must still be a means for releasing the stored energy little by little.

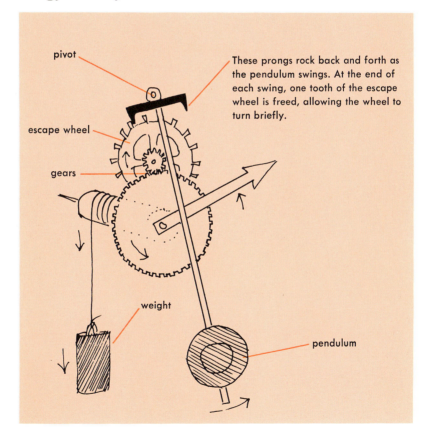

pivot

These prongs rock back and forth as the pendulum swings. At the end of each swing, one tooth of the escape wheel is freed, allowing the wheel to turn briefly.

escape wheel

gears

weight

pendulum

SPRING ENGINES

A spring is not a source of energy. It is a device for *storing* energy. Let's take a bow and arrow, for example, to see how this works. A bow is really nothing more than a large spring. When you pull back on the bowstring, you bend the bow. And as long as you hold the string, the energy is stored in the bow, waiting to send the arrow flying away. When you release the string the bow snaps back to its original shape, and the energy that was stored in it is used to propel the arrow. There is no energy in the bow itself—it is simply a means for storing energy.

Then, where did the energy that sent the arrow on its way come from? It came from your strong right arm, which bent the bow. The bow itself was a way to utilize the energy in that arm.

There are many ways in which energy can be stored. A dam holding back water, ready to turn a turbine, is storing energy. So is the weight in a grandfather clock when it is raised and ready to turn the wheels and gears that move the minute and hour hands.

Rubber is one of the more common materials that have the ability to store energy. A length of rubber acts like a spring. A slingshot—which uses two lengths of rubber—is storing energy when it is pulled taut. A balsa-wood model airplane with a rubber-band motor ·works on the same principle. When you wind up the propeller, twisting the rubber band, you are storing up the energy that will spin the propeller.

SOME RUBBER-BAND MODELS

The stern-wheel boat illustrated below is powered by a rubber band. This is a very simple model to make, and great fun in a bathtub or at the beach. To operate this boat, you turn the paddle wheel until the rubber band is twisted as tight as it will stretch without breaking. Then place the boat in the water and release the paddle wheel. The rubber band will unwind, using its stored energy to spin the wheel and send the boat on its way.

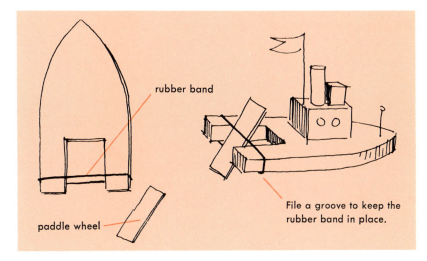

rubber band

paddle wheel

File a groove to keep the rubber band in place.

The spool "tank" shown below operates on a similar principle. The match stick is rotated to wind the rubber band. When it is wound up tight, place the tank on the ground. The unwinding rubber band will then turn the spool, causing it to roll along the ground. If you notch the edges of the spool you will increase its traction, enabling it to climb over rough ground and up slight inclines.

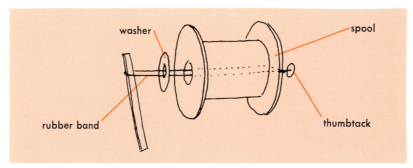

The little airplane shown below can be put together from a few pieces of balsa wood and some odds and ends. This sort of model can also be found in kit form in most toy or ten-cent stores.

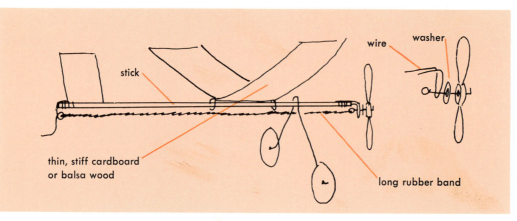

STEEL SPRINGS

The most common spring engine is found in watches and clocks. The spring itself is a long, thin piece of steel. A piece of ordinary mild steel, as in a paper clip, will remain in the shape in which it is bent. But a piece of spring steel is made with special ingredients and treated in such a way that, if bent and then released, it will snap right back to its original shape.

When the long, thin piece of spring steel is wound up into a tight spiral, it tries to unwind back into a straight shape. A clock is simply a mechanism that uses the energy stored in the wound-up spring. There are many wind-up toys that also depend on a spring for their source of power. The drawing below shows in simplified form how a spring engine works.

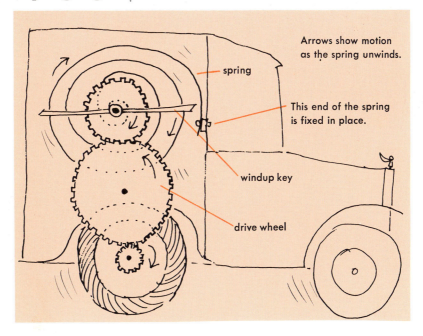

Arrows show motion as the spring unwinds.

spring

This end of the spring is fixed in place.

windup key

drive wheel

This is a train yard, with a whole family of massive locomotives being readied for transcontinental trips. This photograph was taken more than twenty-five years ago. Today most engines are diesel or electric rather than steam.

STEAM ENGINES

So far we have discussed engines that work on energy that is free for the taking. With the water engine, for instance, we simply put a wheel with blades in the path of flowing water. And the wind engine is just placed where a steady breeze will strike it.

But, with the steam engine, things begin to get a little more complicated. The only place to find a steady supply of free steam is, perhaps, at the mouth of a live volcano. And that's no place to put any kind of an engine!

So, the first thing we must obtain for a steam engine is a practical and dependable source of steam. And this, of course, means boiling water. The apparatus in which the water is boiled is called—as you might well guess—a *boiler*. In principle, it is just like a kettle on a stove.

In order to see the power of steam coming from a boiler, try this experiment. Put a kettle partly filled with water on the stove and heat it until a jet of steam comes out the spout. Hold your tin water wheel (as described on page 9) in such a way that the steam strikes its blades. Be careful to keep your fingers away from the steam—it

can give you a bad burn. You'll find that the steam, in escaping from the kettle, provides enough force to keep the wheel spinning quite rapidly.

The sort of boiler that supplies steam to a steam engine is a large and very efficient "kettle." It will produce a great deal of steam under high pressure.

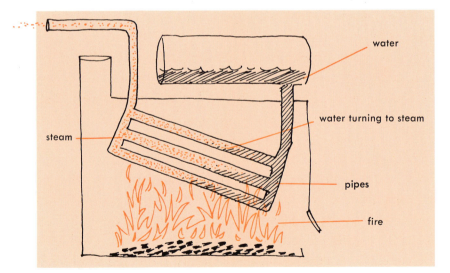

water

water turning to steam

steam

pipes

fire

In a steam engine, the steam passes out of the boiler, through a pipe, past a valve, and into a cylinder. The cylinder is simply a length of pipe sealed at one end and open at the other. Inside this cylinder is a disk called a *piston*. The piston, which can slide up and down in the cylinder, has a rod attached to it.

When the steam rushes into the cylinder, with great force, it pushes against the piston, forcing it down to the far end of the cylinder, as shown below. This is the basic action of a steam engine.

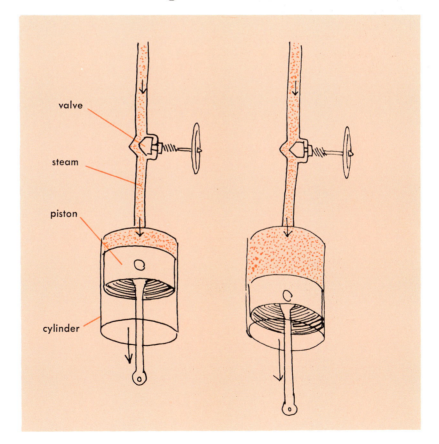

But one push does not make an engine work; there must be a steady, continuous motion. The way this is accomplished is explained in the diagrams below.

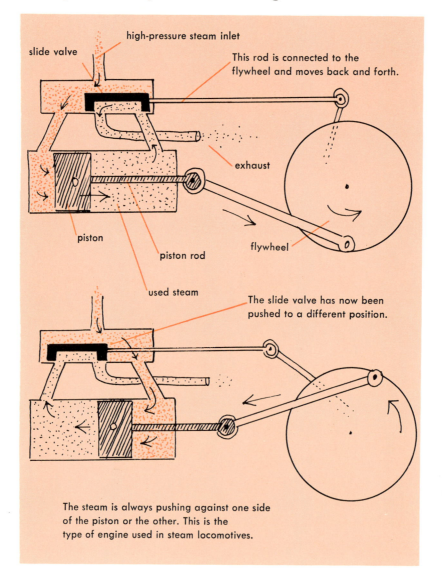

high-pressure steam inlet

slide valve

This rod is connected to the flywheel and moves back and forth.

exhaust

piston

piston rod

flywheel

used steam

The slide valve has now been pushed to a different position.

The steam is always pushing against one side of the piston or the other. This is the type of engine used in steam locomotives.

Here is a dignified old engine built more than half a century ago. Most of the space in it is filled by the boiler. The firebox, where the fuel is burned, is located forward of and below the cab. The cylinder and valve are directly above the two small forward wheels.

STEAM LOCOMOTIVES

A steam locomotive is really nothing more than a steam engine mounted on wheels. The biggest part of the locomotive is the boiler. The cylinders and valve mechanism are on the side, above the front wheels. The photograph above shows a steam locomotive of the sort used in the early 1900's.

The elegant old steam locomotive, with its gleaming bell and polished brass fixtures, is a thing of the past. You are more likely to find one in a museum rather than chugging and puffing its way through the countryside. Today, electric or diesel locomotives are used, because they are more efficient and cheaper to operate.

The sort of steam engine that uses a cylinder and piston has practically disappeared. You might find one in a little backwoods sawmill, or in an ancient ferryboat slowly laboring back and forth across some small stretch of water. And old-time steam engines are occasionally used in some of the undeveloped countries where electricity is unavailable, or gasoline or diesel fuel hard to come by. But there is another type of steam engine, practical and efficient, that is very much in use today. It is called a *steam turbine*.

STEAM TURBINES

A steam turbine is very similar to a water turbine. It is a large wheel with very many thin, curved blades. This kind of steam engine is most often used to turn an electric generator for the production of electricity.

This is the rotating part of a huge steam-driven turbine. Even though it weighs many tons, this rotor must be perfectly balanced in order to ensure smooth, efficient operation with no vibration.

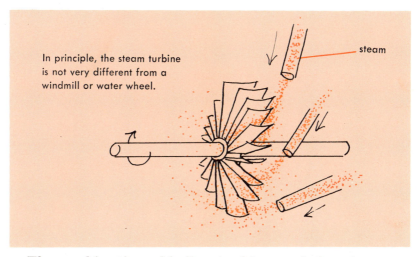

In principle, the steam turbine is not very different from a windmill or water wheel.

steam

The combination of boiler, turbine, and electric generator, as shown below, is typical of the electric power plants that produce the electricity we use. A similar

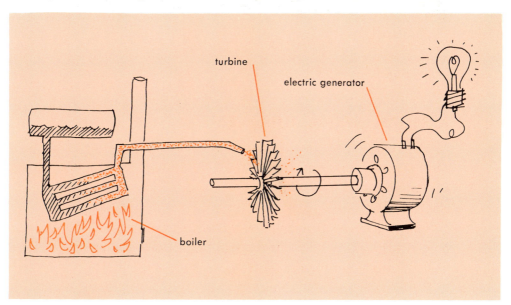

turbine

electric generator

boiler

arrangement is used in atomic power plants and in submarines powered by atomic energy. The only major difference is that the boiler is heated by atomic fuel rather than coal or oil.

Here is the nuclear attack submarine *Gato*, half submerged during a test run. The steam that turns the turbines in this submarine is produced in a boiler that is heated by atomic energy.

A MODEL STEAM TURBINE

The drawing opposite shows a steam turbine engine that you can build with very little trouble. The wheel, or turbine part, is the same as the water wheel already described. The boiler is a 12-ounce juice can. The trick in getting the boiler to work well is to punch two very small holes in the can when you pour out the juice. Use a small nail to punch the holes, positioning them as shown.

Peel the paper label from the empty can and put the can

in a sink full of water to rinse it out. Then fill the can about one-quarter full of water and seal the top hole with a toothpick or splinter of wood.

Position the boiler by means of four large nails, and keep the turbine in place with stiff wire. Use a small can of Sterno to provide the fire. Once the boiler is producing steam, you can adjust your turbine so that the steam strikes the blades at the angle that will produce the most speed.

You can speed up, or slow down, the turbine by varying the amount of heat under the boiler. This can be done by shifting the position of the Sterno can. If your engine is working smoothly, you can bend the end of the shaft into a crank to get a back-and-forth motion. But the engine will not be powerful enough to do any heavy work.

Use your imagination and ingenuity to adapt these models to the materials and tools you have at your disposal. If you understand the principles, you can make an efficient working model, even though it may look quite different from the ones shown.

ELECTRIC MOTORS

The electric motor is one of the most useful tools man has. It does any number of laborsaving tasks. It works the elevators in tall buildings; it powers air-conditioners and turns power tools; it drives water pumps, furnaces, printing presses, and many other kinds of machines. The electric motor is found everywhere, in all sizes and shapes. There is a tiny one in an electric clock. There is a huge one powering a submarine or locomotive.

The fuel, or energy, that makes an electric motor work is electricity. This is a "secondhand" form of energy. It comes from electric generators—which, in turn, are powered by water or steam. For some purposes electricity is best obtained from batteries. The electricity supplied by a battery is the same as the electricity that comes from a house's electric outlet; but in the battery it is produced by chemical action.

Electricity is a complicated thing and not easy to understand, because you can't see or hear or feel it until it is put to work. For practical purposes we can simplify matters by thinking of electricity as small bits of energy —called *electrons*. These can flow through copper wire, just as water flows through a pipe.

However, there is one important difference. Electrons do not flow into one end of a wire and out the other. In order for them to flow at all, they must have a *continuous* path, as shown below. The water pump illustrated would almost immediately run out of water if the pipe did not carry the water all the way around and back into the pump again. And the same is true of a battery or generator. It could not do its job if the electrons did not flow around through the wires and back to their source again. When an electric current flows from a battery or generator, through wires, and then back again, it is called a *complete circuit*.

The electric motor is based on the fact that when electricity is flowing through a wire, an *electromagnetic field* is produced. This field is the same as the one that

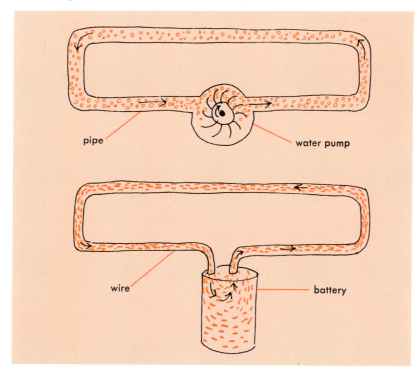

pipe   water pump

wire   battery

surrounds a magnet. You can't see it—but nevertheless it is there. And it is this field that attracts iron and steel.

If we take a long piece of wire through which electricity is flowing, and wind it around a piece of iron, such as a nail, the electromagnetic field becomes quite strong. It can *attract* iron or steel with a good deal of force—and

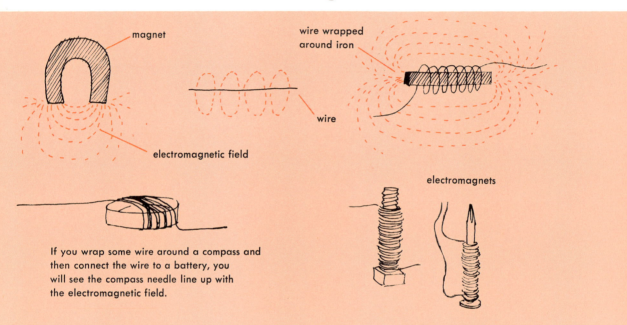

magnet

electromagnetic field

wire wrapped around iron

wire

electromagnets

If you wrap some wire around a compass and then connect the wire to a battery, you will see the compass needle line up with the electromagnetic field.

this is what we are interested in. The coil of wire, with the piece of iron in the center, is called an *electromagnet*. It operates just like an ordinary horseshoe magnet, with one important difference: you can turn it on or off. And you do this simply by connecting—or disconnecting—it from the battery.

You can very easily make an electromagnet yourself. All you need is a battery, a heavy nail or bolt, and some

44

insulated copper wire. "Insulated" wire has a wrapping or covering around it. This keeps the electric current from escaping, or "leaking out," if the wire accidentally touches another wire or the heavy nail.

A MODEL ELECTROMAGNETIC CRANE

The drawing below shows a crane with an electromagnet. The electromagnet can be raised or lowered by means of the crank, and the upper part will turn from one side to the other. A small switch at the base turns the electromagnet on or off. A crane like this is fine for loading or unloading nails, paper clips, or any small metal objects from toy trucks or electric trains.

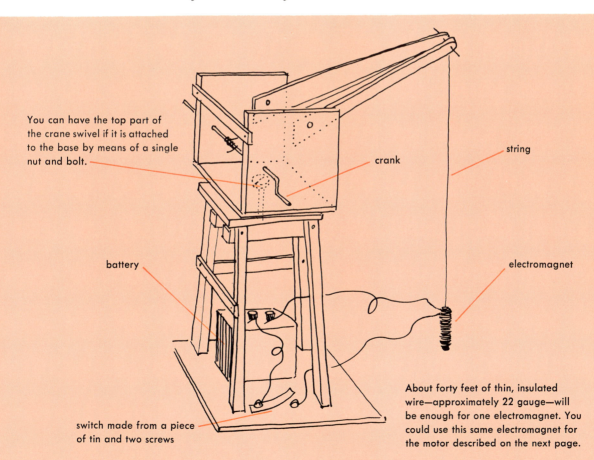

You can have the top part of the crane swivel if it is attached to the base by means of a single nut and bolt.

crank

string

battery

electromagnet

switch made from a piece of tin and two screws

About forty feet of thin, insulated wire—approximately 22 gauge—will be enough for one electromagnet. You could use this same electromagnet for the motor described on the next page.

AN ELECTRIC MOTOR YOU CAN MAKE

The electromagnet is the basic part of all electric motors—and it is the heart of the little motor described here. The spool, with the screws projecting, spins around because the screws are attracted by the electromagnet, one after another. In this motor the electromagnet is not

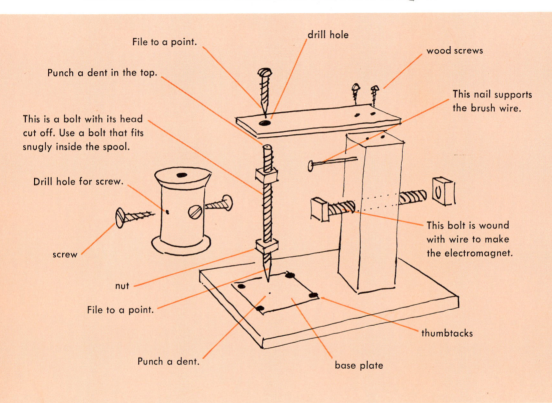

File to a point.

drill hole

wood screws

Punch a dent in the top.

This nail supports the brush wire.

This is a bolt with its head cut off. Use a bolt that fits snugly inside the spool.

Drill hole for screw.

This bolt is wound with wire to make the electromagnet.

screw

nut

File to a point.

thumbtacks

Punch a dent.

base plate

working all the time. It goes off and on, and the current flows only for brief moments. The current begins when the "brush" wire makes contact with the corner of the square nut at the top of the spool. When this little wire and the nut are touching, the circuit is complete, and the

46

electromagnet is "pulling" one of the screws. This is the path the current follows:

1. The current flows out of the battery and goes to the brush wire.

2. The brush wire touches the corner of the nut.

3. The current flows through the nut, down through the center bolt, and into the base plate.

4. From here it goes through the electromagnet, which attracts the screw on the spool. This causes the spool to rotate. (The screw comes close to the electromagnet, but never actually touches it.)

5. The current returns to the battery.

The spool continues to rotate steadily because the circuit is broken as the screw approaches the electromagnet. The corner of the square nut has passed by the brush wire, and there is a gap there now—the circuit is not complete. However, the spool has been given a little pull. It has some momentum, and it continues to revolve. And

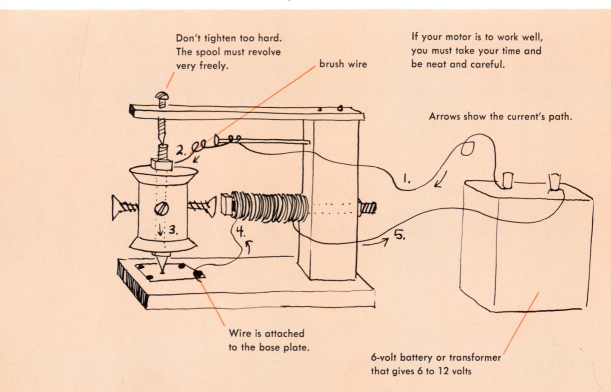

Don't tighten too hard. The spool must revolve very freely.

brush wire

If your motor is to work well, you must take your time and be neat and careful.

Arrows show the current's path.

Wire is attached to the base plate.

6-volt battery or transformer that gives 6 to 12 volts

as it revolves, the next corner of the square nut touches the brush wire. The circuit is once again complete, current flows, and the next screw is pulled toward the electromagnet. This action is so fast, once the motor is started, that all you will see is the spinning spool and some little sparks produced where the brush wire touches the square nut.

If you build this motor, be very careful to see that the brush wire is positioned so that the circuit is broken *just* as one of the screws swings past the electromagnet. You will have to do some delicate adjusting until you get the timing exactly right.

Your motor won't do any practical work, because it is much too small and inefficient. But if it is carefully made and properly adjusted, it will spin around at a great rate of speed, humming and sparking in the merriest way.

A BUZZER

Another kind of electric motor is a buzzer. This engine won't produce a turning or rotating motion, like most of the other engines we've discussed so far—but then, we don't always need or want this kind of motion. For example, the action needed to ring a bell or make a buzzing sound is a back-and-forth action.

The buzzer shown opposite can be made with exactly the same kind of electromagnet used in the spool motor. However, the action is in the spring arm that moves up and down over the electromagnet.

What makes this buzzer buzz is the contact point. When the spring arm is pulled down by the electromagnet, the

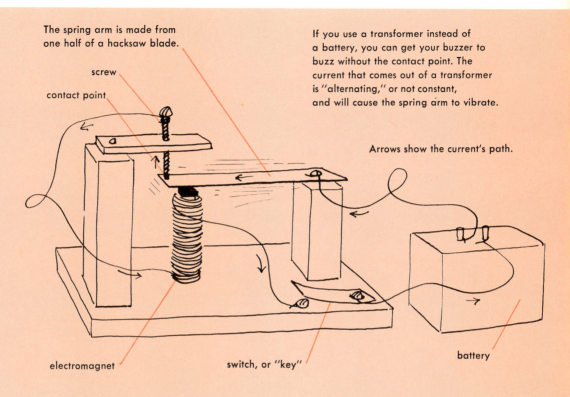

The spring arm is made from one half of a hacksaw blade.

screw

contact point

If you use a transformer instead of a battery, you can get your buzzer to buzz without the contact point. The current that comes out of a transformer is "alternating," or not constant, and will cause the spring arm to vibrate.

Arrows show the current's path.

electromagnet

switch, or "key"

battery

contact between the contact point and the spring arm is broken. Now there is a gap; the circuit is no longer complete, and the electromagnet no longer pulls the movable arm. When this happens, the arm springs back up to its former position—making contact again. Then the entire action is repeated. The arm moves up and down at a very fast rate of speed, producing a buzzing sound.

GASOLINE ENGINES

A source of energy that is much used these days is found deep underground. It is oil, or petroleum. It comes from the decayed remains of tiny animals and plants that lived hundreds of millions of years ago. These substances were trapped deep in the ground and under tremendous pressure. Through the centuries, they gradually changed in their chemical composition until they became petroleum. When petroleum is pumped out of the ground and then treated in various ways, it ends up as gasoline.

Like dynamite or TNT, gasoline is a very explosive material. If a spark or a match is touched to even a little gasoline, it will burn with a huge *whoosh* of flame and heat. It is this explosive energy that is used in the gasoline engines found in most modern cars, buses, and trucks.

On the way from the gas tank to the engine, the gasoline passes through a complicated gadget called a *carburetor*. The carburetor mixes the gasoline with air. This makes the gasoline much more explosive.

The actual burning, or exploding, of the gasoline-air mixture takes place inside a cylinder, and it is touched off by an electric spark. The burning produces gases that are under enormous pressure—and it is this pressure that pushes down the piston. In many ways the gasoline engine is similar to the steam engine. Both have a cylinder in which a piston slides up and down.

50

The diagrams below show the movements of the different parts of the engine at various times.

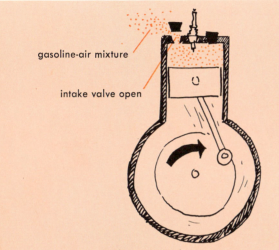

gasoline-air mixture

intake valve open

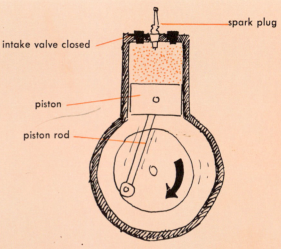

spark plug

intake valve closed

piston

piston rod

1. At this moment the piston is moving downward inside the cylinder. The intake valve is open, so that the gasoline-air mixture can pass into the cylinder.

2. The crankshaft has made a half turn. The piston is now on its way back up the cylinder. The intake valve is closed. The gasoline-air mixture is being squeezed, or compressed. This makes it still more explosive.

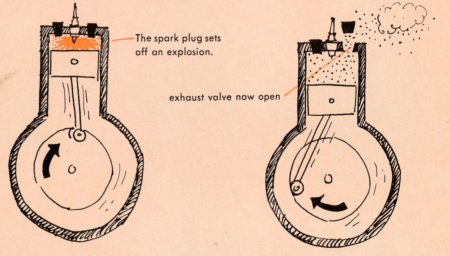

The spark plug sets off an explosion.

exhaust valve now open

3. Bang! An electric charge from the spark plug now sets off the explosion. Like all explosions, this one is simply a very rapid, violent burning action. It causes the expansion of the gasoline-air mixture, creating the pressure that does the work by pushing down the piston.

4. The crankshaft has made another half turn, and the piston is now on its way back up again. But now the exhaust valve is open. As the piston moves upward, it pushes the burned gases past this valve and out of the cylinder. And now we are ready to repeat the entire process.

The timing and sequence of these actions is critical, and quite complicated. Many gears and levers not shown in the diagrams are needed to make the valves open and close at exactly the right moment. And the spark plug must be timed so as to give off its spark just when needed. All of these things, of course, happen very quickly. There are thousands of "explosions" every minute.

Most engines have more than one cylinder. The usual automobile engine has between four and eight cylinders—and each cylinder fires at a slightly different time from the others, so that there is a regular and continuous series of impulses and a steady, smooth source of power.

This is an eight-cylinder (V-8) diesel engine. It looks very much like a gasoline engine and is used in large trucks.

There are a great many variations of the gasoline engine. There are diesel engines, which use a different kind of fuel. There are little, one-cylinder engines of the sort used in lawn mowers and small outboard motors. There are V-8 engines, and the old-fashioned airplane engine with the cylinders mounted in a circle surrounding the crankshaft. But in all these engines, the fundamental action is the same: an explosive expansion of gases pushes down a piston that is connected to a crankshaft.

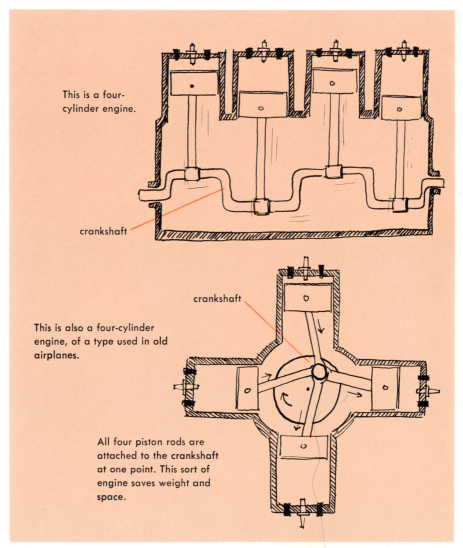

This is a four-cylinder engine.

crankshaft

crankshaft

This is also a four-cylinder engine, of a type used in old airplanes.

All four piston rods are attached to the crankshaft at one point. This sort of engine saves weight and space.

The Air Force F-100 is one of the fastest United States jet planes. The air intake is at the very front, and the exhaust at the tail. The F-100 has gone 755 miles an hour, which is considerably faster than the speed of sound.

JET AND ROCKET ENGINES

If you take a balloon, blow it full of air, and then let it go without tying the end, it will fly about at a great rate until all the air is used up. The balloon is a simple jet engine; it is working on exactly the same principle as the large jet engine in a supersonic aircraft. This basic

principle is that every action produces an equal and opposite reaction. This may sound like a difficult idea, but it really isn't. Think of it as shown below.

When you push the dummy it will move backward. But *your* body is also pushed backward—in the opposite direction. The action of the dummy (moving to the right) has an equal and opposite reaction on your body (moving to the left.)

You can see the same thing with a rifle or cannon. The shell flies off to the right. But there is a "kick," or recoil of the gun itself, which is to the left. The force pushing the shell to the right is equal to the force pushing the gun to the left. The gun doesn't move any great distance, however, because it is so heavy in comparison with the shell.

With the balloon, the escaping air is thrust in one direction—and the balloon itself is thrust in the opposite direction. If there were some way to keep it from running out of air, the balloon would make a small, but speedy, jet engine.

An airplane jet engine is like a balloon that never runs out of air. The jet engine is open at *both* ends. Air comes in the front end, as shown in the diagram below, and is expelled with great force from the other end.

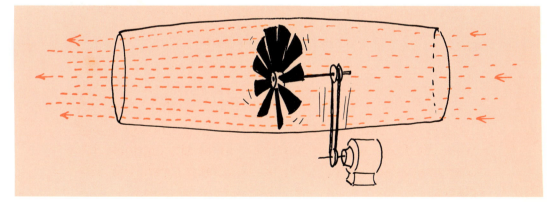

A turbojet engine, of the sort shown below, is slightly more complicated than a simple tube with a fan in the center. In this engine, there are two sets of fan blades. The set to the rear are turned by the action of the burning fuel (which is usually kerosene). The burning gases from the fuel strike the blades of the fan, just as in a steam or water turbine. This causes the turbine to turn.

The turbine is connected by means of a long shaft to another set of fan blades, located at the front end of the engine. These fan blades take the air coming in the front, compress it, and speed up its flow.

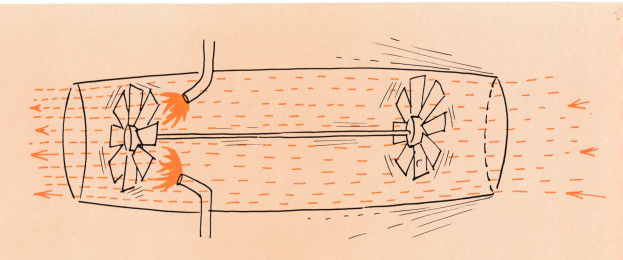

Then the compressed air, together with the hot gases from the fuel, is thrust out the rear of the engine with tremendous force. This thrust is what propels the airplane.

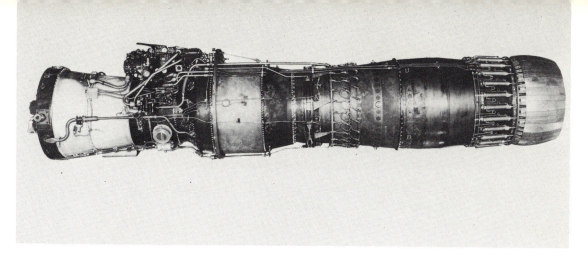

This is a turbojet engine. It is used in several Navy and Air Force fighter planes, and is the power source for the F-100. The air intake is on the right.

A rocket engine works on the same principle as the jet engine, except that it doesn't take in air as it moves— it carries its own air supply right along with it instead. Because a rocket engine doesn't depend on the air around it, it can fly beyond the atmosphere of the earth. The earth has a layer of air surrounding it for less than a hundred miles. Beyond this there is empty space. And that is why the engines used to send satellites into outer space are rocket engines rather than jet engines.

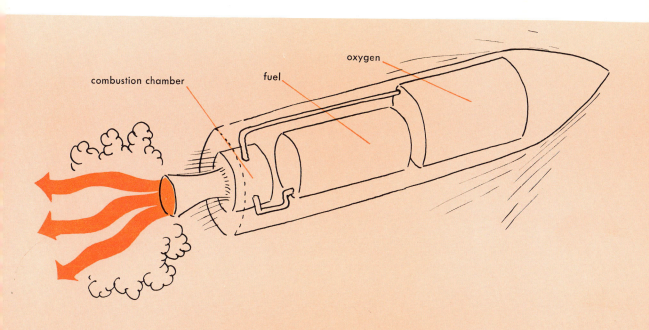

combustion chamber   fuel   oxygen

A rocket engine carries its fuel (such as kerosene), as shown on the preceding page. However, no fuel will burn without oxygen. So the rocket also carries a supply of oxygen. The fuel and the oxygen meet and burn in the *combustion chamber*, producing the blast of expanding gases that propels the rocket. A great many scientists today are experimenting with different kinds of rockets, and with different fuels, in an effort to develop still more powerful rocket engines. Soon there will be a rocket that will take a man to the moon—and some day there may be one that will take him even beyond that.

Here is the booster, or first stage, of the Saturn rocket, which launched the first Apollo spacecraft. You can see the nozzles (which have a temporary protective cap) of the eight engines. Each one of these engines delivers 188,000 pounds of thrust.

THE FUTURE

Man is a creature with a great deal of curiosity. He has always looked about him, noticed the energy contained in the natural world, and wondered how he might use it. Benjamin Franklin saw the flashing of lightning in the clouds; and he wondered if this might not be a form of energy that could be put to some practical use. Thomas Fulton looked at the steam coming out of a kettle of boiling water; and he wondered how the energy of steam might be used to propel a boat.

And yet, there are still many energy sources that are not now being put to work. One example is the tides. These are an enormously powerful force. All the water in the oceans rises and falls twice each day. Think of the weight of all that water, and what it could do if harnessed! And yet no one has thought of any practical way of using it.

Or the sun! As we have seen, this is the most basic source of energy. But we usually use it very indirectly. There is one way, however, that you have probably used it directly—and that is with a magnifying glass. A magnifying glass will concentrate the heat of the sun to a sharp point, at which it is strong enough to set a leaf or a piece of paper on fire.

There are some machines, such as solar batteries and solar house-heating furnaces, that have already been invented to take advantage of the energy in the sun's rays. But these are rather specialized, and not of much really practical use. Probably the most practical *direct* use of the sun, so far, is hanging out clothes to dry!

There are many other energy sources available that will no doubt be used in the future. Who knows—perhaps someday you will read about a man who has invented a snowflake motor, or a growing-grass engine, or a machine that is operated by starlight.

ABOUT THE AUTHOR

When Harvey Weiss was asked about MOTORS AND ENGINES AND HOW THEY WORK, he said: "I adore motors and engines—particularly the simpler kind, where things turn and shuttle and spark and vibrate. Motors and engines today are too efficient and mysterious. You can't *see* anything when you look at them—just a smooth housing that hides all the fun. I think the old steam locomotives with their steam and oil and hissing and clanging were enormously exciting. So were all the other early, simple motors and engines. I've enjoyed working on this book because its descriptions of the actions of motors and engines evoke all this, and because the models described in the book do actually perform in this very simple and apparent and quite beautiful way."

A well-known sculptor whose work has been exhibited in many museums throughout the country, Mr. Weiss is a dedicated tinkerer as well as a writer and illustrator of numerous books for boys and girls.